PENGUIN BOOKS

Published by the Penguin Group. Penguin Books Ltd, 27 Wrights Lane, London w8 5tz, England. Penguin Books USA Inc., 375 Hudson Street, New York, New York 10014, USA. Penguin Books Australia Ltd, Ringwood, Victoria, Australia. Penguin Books Canada Ltd, 10 Alcorn Avenue, Toronto, Ontario, Canada m4v 3b2. Penguin Books (NZ) Ltd, 182–190 Wairau Road, Auckland 10, New Zealand · Penguin Books Ltd, Registered Offices: Harmondsworth, Middlesex, England · **This is the first chapter of** *Sexual Personae: Art and Decadence from Nefertiti to Emily Dickinson* **by Camille Paglia, published by Penguin Books in 1992. This edition published 1995** · Copyright © Yale University, 1990. All rights reserved · The moral right of the author has been asserted · Typeset by Datix International Limited, Bungay, Suffolk. Printed in England by Clays Ltd, St Ives plc · Except in the United States of America, this book is sold subject to the condition that it shall not, by way of trade or otherwise, be lent, re-sold, hired out, or otherwise circulated without the publisher's prior consent in any form of binding or cover other than that in which it is published and without a similar condition including this condition being imposed on the subsequent purchaser · 10 9 8 7 6 5 4 3 2 1

In the beginning was nature. The background from which and against which our ideas of God were formed, nature remains the supreme moral problem. We cannot hope to understand sex and gender until we clarify our attitude toward nature. Sex is a subset to nature. Sex is the natural in man.

Society is an artificial construction, a defense against nature's power. Without society, we would be storm-tossed on the barbarous sea that is nature. Society is a system of inherited forms reducing our humiliating passivity to nature. We may alter these forms, slowly or suddenly, but no change in society will change nature. Human beings are not nature's favorites. We are merely one of a multitude of species upon which nature indiscriminately exerts its force. Nature has a master agenda we can only dimly know.

Human life began in flight and fear. Religion rose from rituals of propitiation, spells to lull the punishing elements. To this day, communities are few in regions scorched by heat or shackled by ice. Civilized man conceals from himself the extent of his subordination to nature. The grandeur of culture, the consolation of religion absorb his attention and win his faith. But let nature shrug, and all is in ruin. Fire, flood, lightning, tornado, hurricane, volcano, earthquake – anywhere at any time. Disaster falls upon the good and bad. Civilized life requires a state of illusion. The idea of the ultimate benevolence of nature and God is the most potent of man's survival mechanisms. Without it, culture would revert to fear and despair.

Sexuality and eroticism are the intricate intersection of nature and culture. Feminists grossly oversimplify the problem of sex when they reduce it to a matter of social convention: readjust society, eliminate sexual inequality, purify sex roles, and happiness and harmony will reign. Here feminism, like all liberal movements of the past two hundred years, is heir to Rousseau. *The Social Contract* (1762) begins: 'Man is born free, and everywhere he is in chains.' Pitting benign Romantic nature against corrupt society, Rousseau produced the progressivist strain in nineteenth-century culture, for which social reform was the means to achieve paradise on earth. The bubble of these hopes was burst by the catastrophes of two world wars. But Rousseauism was reborn in the postwar generation of the Sixties, from which contemporary feminism developed.

Rousseau rejects original sin, Christianity's pessimistic view of man born unclean, with a propensity for evil. Rousseau's idea, derived from Locke, of man's innate goodness led to social environmentalism, now the dominant ethic of American human services, penal codes, and behaviorist therapies. It assumes that aggression, violence, and crime come from social deprivation – a poor neighborhood, a bad home. Thus feminism blames rape on pornography and, by a smug circularity of reasoning, interprets outbreaks of sadism as a backlash to itself. But rape and sadism have been evident throughout history and, at some moment, in all cultures.

This book takes the point of view of Sade, the most unread major writer in western literature. Sade's work is a comprehensive satiric critique of Rousseau, written in the decade after the first failed Rousseauist experiment, the French Revolution, which ended not in political paradise but in the hell of the Reign of Terror. Sade follows Hobbes rather than Locke. Aggression

2

comes from nature; it is what Nietzsche is to call the will-to-power. For Sade, getting back to nature (the Romantic imperative that still permeates our culture from sex counseling to cereal commercials) would be to give free rein to violence and lust. I agree. Society is not the criminal but the force which keeps crime in check. When social controls weaken, man's innate cruelty bursts forth. The rapist is created not by bad social influences but by a failure of social conditioning. Feminists, seeking to drive power relations out of sex, have set themselves against nature. Sex *is* power. Identity is power. In western culture, there are no nonexploitative relationships. Everyone has killed in order to live. Nature's universal law of creation from destruction operates in mind as in matter. As Freud, Nietzsche's heir, asserts, identity is conflict. Each generation drives its plow over the bones of the dead.

Modern liberalism suffers unresolved contradictions. It exalts individualism and freedom and, on its radical wing, condemns social orders as oppressive. On the other hand, it expects government to provide materially for all, a feat manageable only by an expansion of authority and a swollen bureaucracy. In other words, liberalism defines government as tyrant father but demands it behave as nurturant mother. Feminism has inherited these contradictions. It sees every hierarchy as repressive, a social fiction; every negative about woman is a male lie designed to keep her in her place. Feminism has exceeded its proper mission of seeking political equality for women and has ended by rejecting contingency, that is, human limitation by nature or fate.

Sexual freedom, sexual liberation. A modern delusion. We are hierarchical animals. Sweep one hierarchy away, and another will take its place, perhaps less palatable than the first. There are 3 hierarchies in nature and alternate hierarchies in society. In nature, brute force is the law, a survival of the fittest. In society, there are protections for the weak. Society is our frail barrier against nature. When the prestige of state and religion is low, men are free, but they find freedom intolerable and seek new ways to enslave themselves, through drugs or depression. My theory is that whenever sexual freedom is sought or achieved, sadomasochism will not be far behind. Romanticism always turns into decadence. Nature is a hard taskmaster. It is the hammer and the anvil, crushing individuality. Perfect freedom would be to die by earth, air, water, and fire.

Sex is a far darker power than feminism has admitted. Behaviorist sex therapies believe guiltless, no-fault sex is possible. But sex has always been girt round with taboo, irrespective of culture. Sex is the point of contact between man and nature, where morality and good intentions fall to primitive urges. I called it an intersection. This intersection is the uncanny crossroads of Hecate, where all things return in the night. Eroticism is a realm stalked by ghosts. It is the place beyond the pale, both cursed and enchanted.

This book shows how much in culture goes against our best wishes. Integration of man's body and mind is a profound problem that is not about to be solved by recreational sex or an expansion of women's civil rights. Incarnation, the limitation of mind by matter, is an outrage to imagination. Equally outrageous is gender, which we have not chosen but which nature has imposed upon us. Our physicality is torment, our body the tree of nature on which Blake sees us crucified.

Sex is daemonic. This term, current in Romantic studies of the past twenty-five years, derives from the Greek *daimon*, meaning a spirit of lower divinity than the Olympian gods

4

(hence my pronunciation 'daimonic'). The outcast Oedipus becomes a daemon at Colonus. The word came to mean a man's guardian shadow. Christianity turned the daemonic into the demonic. The Greek daemons were not evil – or rather they were both good and evil, like nature itself, in which they dwelled. Freud's unconscious is a daemonic realm. In the day we are social creatures, but at night we descend to the dream world where nature reigns, where there is no law but sex, cruelty, and metamorphosis. Day itself is invaded by daemonic night. Moment by moment, night flickers in the imagination, in eroticism, subverting our strivings for virtue and order, giving an uncanny aura to objects and persons, revealed to us through the eyes of the artist.

The ghost-ridden character of sex is implicit in Freud's brilliant theory of 'family romance'. We each have an incestuous constellation of sexual personae that we carry from childhood to the grave and that determines whom and how we love or hate. Every encounter with friend or foe, every clash with or submission to authority bears the perverse traces of family romance. Love is a crowded theater, for as Harold Bloom remarks, 'We can never embrace (sexually or otherwise) a single person, but embrace the whole of her or his family romance.'* We still know next to nothing of the mystery of cathexis, the investment of libido in certain people or things. The element of free will in sex and emotion is slight. As poets know, falling in love is irrational.

Like art, sex is fraught with symbols. Family romance means that adult sex is always representation, ritualistic acting out of vanished realities. A perfectly humane eroticism may be impossible. Somewhere in every family romance is hostility and

* The Anxiety of Influence: A Theory of Poetry (New York, 1973), 94.   5

aggression, the homicidal wishes of the unconscious. Children are monsters of unbridled egotism and will, for they spring directly from nature, hostile intimations of immorality. We carry that daemonic will within us forever. Most people conceal it with acquired ethical precepts and meet it only in their dreams, which they hastily forget upon waking. The will-to-power is innate, but the sexual scripts of family romance are learned. Human beings are the only creatures in whom consciousness is so entangled with animal instinct. In western culture, there can never be a purely physical or anxiety-free sexual encounter. Every attraction, every pattern of touch, every orgasm is shaped by psychic shadows.

The search for freedom through sex is doomed to failure. In sex, compulsion and ancient Necessity rule. The sexual personae of family romance are obliterated by the tidal force of regression, the backwards movement toward primeval dissolution, which Ferenczi identifies with ocean. An orgasm is a domination, a surrender, or a breaking through. Nature is no respecter of human identity. This is why so many men turn away or flee after sex, for they have sensed the annihilation of the daemonic. Western love is a displacement of cosmic realities. It is a defense mechanism rationalizing forces ungoverned and ungovernable. Like early religion, it is a device enabling us to control our primal fear.

Sex cannot be understood because nature cannot be understood. Science is a method of logical analysis of nature's operations. It has lessened human anxiety about the cosmos by demonstrating the materiality of nature's forces, and their frequent predictability. But science is always playing catch-up ball. Nature breaks its own rules whenever it wants. Science cannot avert a single thunderbolt. Western science is a product of the

Apollonian mind: its hope is that by naming and classification, by the cold light of intellect, archaic night can be pushed back and defeated.

Name and person are part of the west's quest for form. The west insists on the discrete identity of objects. To name is to know; to know is to control. I will demonstrate that the west's greatness arises from this delusional certitude. Far Eastern culture has never striven against nature in this way. Compliance, not confrontation is its rule. Buddhist meditation seeks the unity and harmony of reality. Twentieth-century physics, going full circle back to Heracleitus, postulates that all matter is in motion. In other words, there is no thing, only energy. But this perception has not been imaginatively absorbed, for it cancels the west's intellectual and moral assumptions.

The westerner knows by seeing. Perceptual relations are at the heart of our culture, and they have produced our titanic contributions to art. Walking in nature, we see, identify, name, *recognize*. This recognition is our apotropaion, that is, our warding off of fear. Recognition is ritual cognition, a repetition-compulsion. We say that nature is beautiful. But this aesthetic judgment, which not all peoples have shared, is another defense formation, woefully inadequate for encompassing nature's totality. What is pretty in nature is confined to the thin skin of the globe upon which we huddle. Scratch that skin, and nature's daemonic ugliness will erupt.

Our focus on the pretty is an Apollonian strategy. The leaves and flowers, the birds, the hills are a patchwork pattern by which we map the known. What the west represses in its view of nature is the chthonian, which means 'of the earth' – but earth's bowels, not its surface. Jane Harrison uses the term for pre-Olympian Greek religion, and I adopt it as a substitute for

Dionysian, which has become contaminated with vulgar pleasantries. The Dionysian is no picnic. It is the chthonian realities which Apollo evades, the blind grinding of subterranean force, the long slow suck, the murk and ooze. It is the dehumanizing brutality of biology and geology, the Darwinian waste and bloodshed, the squalor and rot we must block from consciousness to retain our Apollonian integrity as persons. Western science and aesthetics are attempts to revise this horror into imaginatively palatable form.

The daemonism of chthonian nature is the west's dirty secret. Modern humanists made the 'tragic sense of life' the touchstone of mature understanding. They defined man's mortality and the transience of time as literature's supreme subjects. In this I again see evasion and even sentimentality. The tragic sense of life is a partial response to experience. It is a reflex of the west's resistance to and misapprehension of nature, compounded by the errors of liberalism, which in its Romantic nature-philosophy has followed the Rousseauist Wordsworth rather than the daemonic Coleridge.

Tragedy is the most western literary genre. It did not appear in Japan until the late nineteenth century. The western will, setting itself up against nature, dramatized its own inevitable fall as a human universal, which it is not. An irony of literary history is the birth of tragedy in the cult of Dionysus. The protagonist's destruction recalls the slaughter of animals and, even earlier, of real human beings in archaic ritual. It is no accident that tragedy as we know it dates from the Apollonian fifth century of Athens' greatness, whose cardinal work is Aeschylus' *Oresteia*, a celebration of the defeat of chthonian power. Drama, a Dionysian mode, turned against Dionysus in making the passage from ritual to mimesis, that is, from action to representation. Aristotle's 'pity and fear' is a broken promise, a plea for vision without horror.

Few Greek tragedies fully conform to the humanist commentary on them. Their barbaric residue will not come unglued. Even in the fifth century, as we shall see, a satiric response to Apollonianized theater came in Euripides' decadent plays. Problems in accurate assessment of Greek tragedy include not only the loss of three-quarters of the original body of work but the lack of survival of any complete satyr-play. This was the finale to the classic trilogy, an obscene comic burlesque. In Greek tragedy, comedy always had the last word. Modern criticism has projected a Victorian and, I feel, Protestant high seriousness upon pagan culture that still blankets teaching of the humanities. Paradoxically, assent to savage chthonian realities leads not to gloom but to humor. Hence Sade's strange laughter, his wit amid the most fantastic cruelties. For life is not a tragedy but a comedy. Comedy is born of the clash between Apollo and Dionysus. Nature is always pulling the rug out from under our pompous ideals.

Female tragic protagonists are rare. Tragedy is a male paradigm of rise and fall, a graph in which dramatic and sexual climax are in shadowy analogy. Climax is another western invention. Traditional eastern stories are picaresque, horizontal chains of incident. There is little suspense or sense of an ending. The sharp vertical peaking of western narrative, as later of orchestral music, is exemplified by Sophocles' *Oedipus Rex*, whose moment of maximum intensity Aristotle calls *peripeteia*, reversal. Western dramatic climax was produced by the agon of male will. Through action to identity. Action is the route of escape from nature, but all action circles back to origins, the womb-tomb of nature. Oedipus, trying to escape his mother, runs straight into her arms. Western narrative is a mystery story, a process of detection. But since what is detected is unbearable, every revelation leads to another repression.

The major women of tragedy – Euripides' Medea and Phaedra, Shakespeare's Cleopatra and Lady Macbeth, Racine's Phèdre – skew the genre by their disruptive relation to male action. Tragic woman is less moral than man. Her will-to-power is naked. Her actions are under a chthonian cloud. They are a conduit of the irrational, opening the genre to intrusions of the barbaric force that drama shut out at its birth. Tragedy is a western vehicle for testing and purification of the male will. The difficulty in grafting female protagonists onto it is a result not of male prejudice but of instinctive sexual strategics. Woman introduces untransformed cruelty into tragedy because she is the problem that the genre is trying to correct.

Tragedy plays a male game, a game it invented to snatch victory from the jaws of defeat. It is not flawed choice, flawed action, or even death itself which is the ultimate human dilemma. The gravest challenge to our hopes and dreams is the messy biological business-as-usual that is going on within us and without us at every hour of every day. Consciousness is a pitiful hostage of its flesh-envelope, whose surges, circuits, and secret murmurings it cannot stay or speed. This is the chthonian drama that has no climax but only an endless round, cycle upon cycle. Microcosm mirrors macrocosm. Free will is stillborn in the red cells of our body, for there is no free will in nature. Our choices come to us pre-packaged and special delivery, molded by hands not our own.

Tragedy's inhospitality to woman springs from nature's inhospitality to man. The identification of woman with nature was universal in prehistory. In hunting or agrarian societies dependent upon nature, femaleness was honored as an immanent principle of fertility. As culture progressed, crafts and commerce supplied a concentration of resources freeing men from the caprices of weather or the handicap of geography. With nature at one remove, femaleness receded in importance.

Buddhist cultures retained the ancient meanings of femaleness long after the west renounced them. Male and female, the Chinese yang and yin, are balanced and interpenetrating powers in man and nature, to which society is subordinate. This code of passive acceptance has its roots in India, a land of sudden extremes where a monsoon can wipe out 50,000 people overnight. The femaleness of fertility religions is always double-edged. The Indian nature-goddess Kali is creator *and* destroyer, granting boons with one set of arms while cutting throats with the other. She is the lady ringed with skulls. The moral ambivalence of the great mother goddesses has been conveniently forgotten by those American feminists who have resurrected them. We cannot grasp nature's bare blade without shedding our own blood.

Western culture from the start has swerved from femaleness. The last major western society to worship female powers was Minoan Crete. And significantly, that fell and did not rise again. The immediate cause of its collapse – quake, plague, or invasion – is beside the point. The lesson is that cultic femaleness is no guarantee of cultural strength or viability. What did survive, what did vanquish circumstance and stamp its mind-set on Europe was Mycenaean warrior culture, descending to us through Homer. The male will-to-power: Mycenaeans from the south and Dorians from the north would fuse to form Apollonian Athens, from which came the Greco-Roman line of western history.

Both the Apollonian and Judeo-Christian traditions are transcendental. That is, they seek to surmount or transcend nature. Despite Greek culture's contrary Dionysian element, which I will discuss, high classicism was an Apollonian achievement. Judaism, Christianity's parent sect, is the most powerful of protests against nature. The Old Testament asserts that a father god made nature and that differentiation into objects and gender was after the fact of his maleness. Judeo-Christianity, like Greek worship of the Olympian gods, is a sky-cult. It is an advanced stage in the history of religion, which everywhere began as earth-cult, veneration of fruitful nature.

The evolution from earth-cult to sky-cult shifts woman into the nether realm. Her mysterious procreative powers and the resemblance of her rounded breasts, belly, and hips to earth's contours put her at the center of early symbolism. She was the model for the Great Mother figures who crowded the birth of religion worldwide. But the mother cults did not mean social freedom for women. On the contrary, as I will show in a discussion of Hollywood in the sequel to this book, cult-objects are prisoners of their own symbolic inflation. Every totem lives in taboo.

Woman was an idol of belly-magic. She seemed to swell and give birth by her own law. From the beginning of time, woman has seemed an uncanny being. Man honored but feared her. She was the black maw that had spat him forth and would devour him anew. Men, bonding together, invented culture as a defense against female nature. Sky-cult was the most sophisticated step in this process, for its switch of the creative locus from earth to sky is a shift from belly-magic to head-magic. And from this defensive head-magic has come the spectacular glory of male civilization, which has lifted woman with it. The very language and logic modern woman uses to assail patriarchal culture were the invention of men.

Hence the sexes are caught in a comedy of historical indebtedness. Man, repelled by his debt to a physical mother, created an alternate reality, a heterocosm to give him the illusion of freedom. Woman, at first content to accept man's protections but now inflamed with desire for her own illusory freedom, invades man's systems and suppresses her indebtedness to him as she steals them. By head-magic she will deny there ever was a problem of sex and nature. She has inherited the anxiety of influence.

The identification of woman with nature is the most troubled and troubling term in this historical argument. Was it ever true? Can it still be true? Most feminist readers will disagree, but I think this identification not myth but reality. All the genres of philosophy, science, high art, athletics, and politics were invented by men. But by the Promethean law of conflict and capture, woman has a right to seize what she will and to vie with man on his own terms. Yet there is a limit to what she can alter in herself and in man's relation to her. Every human being must wrestle with nature. But nature's burden falls more heavily on one sex. With luck, this will not limit woman's achievement, that is, her action in male-created social space. But it must limit eroticism, that is, our imaginative lives in sexual space, which may overlap social space but is not identical with it.

Nature's cycles are woman's cycles. Biologic femaleness is a sequence of circular returns, beginning and ending at the same point. Woman's centrality gives her a stability of identity. She does not have to become but only to be. Her centrality is a great obstacle to man, whose quest for identity she blocks. He must transform himself into an independent being, that is, a being free of her. If he does not, he will simply fall back into her. Reunion with the mother is a siren call haunting our imagination. Once there was bliss, and now there is struggle. Dim memories of life before the traumatic separation of birth may be the source of Arcadian fantasies of a lost golden age. The western idea of history as a propulsive movement into the future, a progressive or Providential design climaxing in the revelation of a Second Coming, is a male formulation. No woman, I submit, could have coined such an idea, since it is a strategy of evasion of woman's own cyclic nature, in which man dreads being caught. Evolutionary or apocalyptic history is a male wish list with a happy ending, a phallic peak.

Woman does not dream of transcendental or historical escape from natural cycle, since she is that cycle. Her sexual maturity means marriage to the moon, waxing and waning in lunar phases. Moon, month, menses: same word, same world. The ancients knew that woman is bound to nature's calendar, an appointment she cannot refuse. The Greek pattern of free will to hybris to tragedy is a male drama, since woman has never been deluded (until recently) by the mirage of free will. She knows there is no free will, since she is not free. She has no choice but acceptance. Whether she desires motherhood or not, nature yokes her into the brute inflexible rhythm of procreative law. Menstrual cycle is an alarming clock that cannot be stopped until nature wills it.

Woman's reproductive apparatus is vastly more complicated than man's, and still ill-understood. All kinds of things can go wrong or cause distress in going right. Western woman is in an agonistic relation to her own body: for her, biologic normalcy is suffering, and health an illness. Dysmenorrhea, it is argued, is a disease of civilization, since women in tribal cultures have few menstrual complaints. But in tribal life, woman has an extended or collective identity; tribal religion honors nature and subordinates itself to it. It is precisely in advanced western society, which attempts to improve or surpass nature and which holds up individualism and self-realization as a model, that the stark facts of woman's condition emerge with painful clarity. The more woman aims for personal identity and autonomy, the more she develops her imagination, the fiercer will be her struggle with nature – that is, with the intractable physical laws of her own body. And the more nature will punish her: do not dare to be free! for your body does not belong to you.

The female body is a chthonian machine, indifferent to the spirit who inhabits it. Organically, it has one mission, pregnancy, which we may spend a lifetime staving off. Nature cares only for species, never individuals: the humiliating dimensions of this biologic fact are most directly experienced by women, who probably have a greater realism and wisdom than men because of it. Woman's body is a sea acted upon by the month's lunar wave-motion. Sluggish and dormant, her fatty tissues are gorged with water, then suddenly cleansed at hormonal high tide. Edema is our mammalian relapse into the vegetable. Pregnancy demonstrates the deterministic character of woman's sexuality. Every pregnant woman has body and self taken over by a chthonian force beyond her control. In the welcome pregnancy, this is a happy sacrifice. But in the unwanted one, initiated by rape or misadventure, it is a horror. Such unfortunate women look directly into nature's heart of darkness. For a fetus is a benign tumor, a vampire who steals in order to live. The so-called miracle of birth is nature getting her own way.

Every month for women is a new defeat of the will. Menstruation was once called 'the curse', a reference to the expulsion from the Garden, when woman was condemned to labor pains because of Eve's sin. Most early cultures hemmed in menstruating women by ritual taboos. Orthodox Jewish women still purify themselves from menstrual uncleanness in the *mikveh*, a ritual bath. Women have borne the symbolic burden of man's imperfections, his grounding in nature. Menstrual blood is the stain, the birthmark of original sin, the filth that transcendental religion must wash from man. Is this identification merely phobic, merely misogynistic? Or is it possible there is something uncanny about menstrual blood, justifying its attachment to taboo? I will argue that it is not menstrual blood *per se* which disturbs the imagination – unstanchable as that red flood may be – but rather the albumen in the blood, the uterine shreds, placental jellyfish of the female sea. This is the chthonian matrix from which we rose. We have an evolutionary revulsion from slime, our site of biologic origins. Every month, it is woman's fate to face the abyss of time and being, the abyss which is herself.

The Bible has come under fire for making woman the fall guy in man's cosmic drama. But in casting a male conspirator, the serpent, as God's enemy, Genesis hedges and does not take its misogyny far enough. The Bible defensively swerves from God's true opponent, chthonian nature. The serpent is not outside Eve but in her. She is the garden *and* the serpent. Anthony Storr says of witches, 'At a very primitive level, all mothers are phallic.'* The Devil is a woman. Modern emancipation movements, discarding stereotypes impeding woman's social advance, refuse to acknowledge procreation's daemonism. Nature is serpentine, a bed of tangled vines, creepers and crawlers, probing dumb fingers of fetid organic life which Wordsworth taught us to call pretty. Biologists speak of man's reptilian brain, the oldest

16   * *Sexual Deviation* (Harmondsworth, Middlesex, 1964), 63.

part of our upper nervous system, killer survivor of the archaic era. I contend that the premenstrual woman incited to snappishness or rage is hearing signals from the reptilian brain. In her, man's latent perversity is manifest. All hell breaks loose, the hell of chthonian nature that modern humanism denies and represses. In every premenstrual woman struggling to govern her temper, sky-cult wars again with earth-cult.

Mythology's identification of woman with nature is correct. The male contribution to procreation is momentary and transient. Conception is a pinpoint of time, another of our phallic peaks of action, from which the male slides back uselessly. The pregnant woman is daemonically, devilishly complete. As an ontological entity, she needs nothing and no one. I shall maintain that the pregnant woman, brooding for nine months upon her own creation, is the pattern of all solipsism, that the historical attribution of narcissism to women is another true myth. Male bonding and patriarchy were the recourse to which man was forced by his terrible sense of woman's power, her imperviousness, her archetypal confederacy with chthonian nature. Woman's body is a labyrinth in which man is lost. It is a walled garden, the medieval *hortus conclusus*, in which nature works its daemonic sorcery. Woman is the primeval fabricator, the real First Mover. She turns a gob of refuse into a spreading web of sentient being, floating on the snaky umbilical by which she leashes every man.

Feminism has been simplistic in arguing that female archetypes were politically motivated falsehoods by men. The historical repugnance to woman has a rational basis: disgust is reason's proper response to the grossness of procreative nature. Reason and logic are the anxiety-inspired domain of Apollo, premiere god of sky-cult. The Apollonian is harsh and phobic, coldly cutting itself off from nature by its superhuman purity. I shall 17 argue that western personality and western achievement are, for better or worse, largely Apollonian. Apollo's great opponent Dionysus is ruler of the chthonian whose law is procreative femaleness. As we shall see, the Dionysian is liquid nature, a miasmic swamp whose prototype is the still pond of the womb.

We must ask whether the equivalence of male and female in Far Eastern symbolism was as culturally efficacious as the hierarchization of male over female has been in the west. Which system has ultimately benefited women more? Western science and industry have freed women from drudgery and danger. Machines do housework. The pill neutralizes fertility. Giving birth is no longer fatal. And the Apollonian line of western rationality has produced the modern aggressive woman who can think like a man and write obnoxious books. The tension and antagonism in western metaphysics developed human higher cortical powers to great heights. Most of western culture is a distortion of reality. But reality *should* be distorted; that is, imaginatively amended. The Buddhist acquiescence to nature is neither accurate about nature nor just to human potential. The Apollonian has taken us to the stars.

Daemonic archetypes of woman, filling world mythology, represent the uncontrollable nearness of nature. Their tradition passes nearly unbroken from prehistoric idols through literature and art to modern movies. The primary image is the *femme fatale*, the woman fatal to man. The more nature is beaten back in the west, the more the *femme fatale* reappears, as a return of the repressed. She is the spectre of the west's bad conscience about nature. She is the moral ambiguity of nature, a malevolent moon that keeps breaking through our fog of hopeful sentiment.

Feminism dismisses the *femme fatale* as a cartoon and libel. If she ever existed, she was simply a victim of society, resorting to destructive womanly wiles because of her lack of access to political power. The *femme fatale* was a career woman *manquée*, her energies neurotically diverted into the boudoir. By such techniques of demystification, feminism has painted itself into a corner. Sexuality is a murky realm of contradiction and ambivalence. It cannot always be understood by social models, which feminism, as an heir of nineteenth-century utilitarianism, insists on imposing on it. Mystification will always remain the disorderly companion of love and art. Eroticism is mystique; that is, the aura of emotion and imagination around sex. It cannot be 'fixed' by codes of social or moral convenience, whether from the political left or right. For nature's fascism is greater than that of any society. There is a daemonic instability in sexual relations that we may have to accept.

The *femme fatale* is one of the most mesmerizing of sexual personae. She is not a fiction but an extrapolation of biologic realities in women that remain constant. The North American Indian myth of the toothed vagina (*vagina dentata*) is a gruesomely direct transcription of female power and male fear. Metaphorically, every vagina has secret teeth, for the male exits as less than when he entered. The basic mechanics of conception require action in the male but nothing more than passive receptivity in the female. Sex as a natural rather than social transaction, therefore, really is a kind of drain of male energy by female fullness. Physical and spiritual castration is the danger every man runs in intercourse with a woman. Love is the spell by which he puts his sexual fear to sleep. Woman's latent vampirism is not a social aberration but a development of her maternal function, for which nature has equipped her with tiresome thoroughness. For the male, every act of intercourse is a return to the mother and a capitulation to her. For men, sex is a 19 struggle for identity. In sex, the male is consumed and released again by the toothed power that bore him, the female dragon of nature.

The *femme fatale* was produced by the mystique of connection between mother and child. A modern assumption is that sex and procreation are medically, scientifically, intellectually 'manageable'. If we keep tinkering with the social mechanism long enough, every difficulty will disappear. Meanwhile, the divorce rate soars. Conventional marriage, despite its inequities, kept the chaos of libido in check. When the prestige of marriage is low, all the nasty daemonism of sexual instinct pops out. Individualism, the self unconstrained by society, leads to the coarser servitude of constraint by nature. Every road from Rousseau leads to Sade. The mystique of our birth from human mothers is one of the daemonic clouds we cannot dispel by tiny declarations of independence. Apollo can swerve from nature, but he cannot obliterate it. As emotional and sexual beings we go full circle. Old age is a second childhood in which earliest memories revive. Chillingly, comatose patients of any age automatically drift toward the fetal position, from which they have to be pried by nurses. We are tied to our birth by unshakable apparitions of sense-memory.

Rousseauist psychologies like feminism assert the ultimate benevolence of human emotion. In such a system, the *femme fatale* logically has no place. I follow Freud, Nietzsche, and Sade in my view of the amorality of the instinctual life. At some level, all love is combat, a wrestling with ghosts. We are only *for* something by being *against* something else. People who believe they are having pleasant, casual, uncomplex sexual encounters, whether with friend, spouse, or stranger, are blocking from
20 consciousness the tangle of psychodynamics at work, just as they

block the hostile clashings of their dream life. Family romance operates at all times. The *femme fatale* is one of the refinements of female narcissism, of the ambivalent self-directedness that is completed by the birth of a child or by the conversion of spouse or lover into child.

Mothers can be fatal to their sons. It is against the mother that men have erected their towering edifice of politics and sky-cult. She is Medusa, in whom Freud sees the castrating and castrated female pubes. But Medusa's snaky hair is also the writhing vegetable growth of nature. Her hideous grimace is men's fear of the laughter of women. She that gives life also blocks the way to freedom. Therefore I agree with Sade that we have the right to thwart nature's procreative compulsions, through sodomy or abortion. Male homosexuality may be the most valorous of attempts to evade the *femme fatale* and to defeat nature. By turning away from the Medusan mother, whether in honor or detestation of her, the male homosexual is one of the great forgers of absolutist western identity. But of course nature has won, as she always does, by making disease the price of promiscuous sex.

The permanence of the *femme fatale* as a sexual persona is part of the weary weight of eroticism, beneath which both ethics and religion founder. Eroticism is society's soft point, through which it is invaded by chthonian nature. The *femme fatale* can appear as Medusan mother or as frigid nymph, masquing in the brilliant luminosity of Apollonian high glamour. Her cool unreachability beckons, fascinates, and destroys. She is not a neurotic but, if anything, a psychopath. That is, she has an amoral affectlessness, a serene indifference to the suffering of others, which she invites and dispassionately observes as tests of her power. The mystique of the *femme fatale* cannot be perfectly translated into male terms. I will speak at length of the beautiful boy, one of the west's most stunning sexual personae. However, the danger of the *homme fatal*, as embodied in today's boyish male hustler, is that he will leave, disappearing to other loves, other lands. He is a rambler, a cowboy and sailor. But the danger of the *femme fatale* is that *she will stay*, still, placid, and paralyzing. Her remaining is a daemonic burden, the ubiquity of Walter Pater's *Mona Lisa*, who smothers history. She is a thorny symbol of the perversity of sex. She will stick.

We are moving in this chapter toward a theory of beauty. I believe that the aesthetic sense, like everything else thus far, is a swerve from the chthonian. It is a displacement from one area of reality to another, analogous to the shift from earth-cult to sky-cult. Ferenczi speaks of the replacement of animal nose by human eye, because of our upright stance. The eye is peremptory in its judgments. It decides what to see and why. Each of our glances is as much exclusion as inclusion. We select, editorialize, and enhance. Our idea of the pretty is a limited notion that cannot possibly apply to earth's metamorphic underworld, a cataclysmic realm of chthonian violence. We choose not to see this violence on our daily strolls. Every time we say nature is beautiful, we are saying a prayer, fingering our worry beads.

The cool beauty of the *femme fatale* is another transformation of chthonian ugliness. Female animals are usually less beautiful than males. The mother bird's dull feathers are camouflage, protecting the nest from predators. Male birds are creatures of spectacular display, of both plumage and parade, partly to impress females and conquer rivals and partly to divert enemies from the nest. Among humans, male ritual display is just as extreme, but for the first time the female becomes a lavishly beautiful object. Why? The female is adorned not simply to increase her property value, as Marxism would demystifyingly have it, but to assure her desirability. Consciousness has made cowards of us all. Animals do not feel sexual fear, because they are not rational beings. They operate under a pure biologic imperative. Mind, which has enabled humanity to adapt and flourish as a species, has also infinitely complicated our functioning as physical beings. We see too much, and so have to stringently limit our seeing. Desire is besieged on all sides by anxiety and doubt. Beauty, an ecstasy of the eye, drugs us and allows us to act. Beauty is our Apollonian revision of the chthonian.

Nature is a Darwinian spectacle of the eaters and the eaten. All phases of procreation are ruled by appetite: sexual intercourse, from kissing to penetration, consists of movements of barely controlled cruelty and consumption. The long pregnancy of the human female and the protracted childhood of her infant, who is not self-sustaining for seven years or more, have produced the agon of psychological dependency that burdens the male for a lifetime. Man justifiably fears being devoured by woman, who is nature's proxy.

Repression is an evolutionary adaptation permitting us to function under the burden of our expanded consciousness. For what we are conscious of could drive us mad. Crude male slang speaks of female genitalia as 'slash' or 'gash'. Freud notes that Medusa turns men to stone because, at first sight, a boy thinks female genitals a wound, from which the penis has been cut. They are indeed a wound, but it is the infant who has been cut away, by violence: the umbilical is a hawser sawed through by a social rescue party. Sexual necessity drives man back to that bloody scene, but he cannot approach it without tremors of apprehension. These he conceals by euphemisms of love and beauty. However, the less well-bred he is — that is, the less socialized — the sharper his sense of the animality of sex and the grosser his language. The foulmouthed roughneck is produced not by society's sexism but by society's absence. For nature is the most foulmouthed of us all.

Woman's current advance in society is not a voyage from myth to truth but from myth to new myth. The rise of rational, technological woman may demand the repression of unpleasant archetypal realities. Ferenczi remarks, 'The periodic pulsations in feminine sexuality (puberty, the menses, pregnancies and parturitions, the climacterium) require a much more powerful repression on the woman's part than is necessary for the man.'[*] In its argument with male society, feminism must suppress the monthly evidence of woman's domination by chthonian nature. Menstruation and childbirth are an affront to beauty and form. In aesthetic terms, they are spectacles of frightful squalor. Modern life, with its hospitals and paper products, has distanced and sanitized these primitive mysteries, just as it has done with death, which used to be a gruelling at-home affair. An awful lot is being swept under the rug: the awe and terror that is our lot.

The woundlike rawness of female genitals is a symbol of the unredeemability of chthonian nature. In aesthetic terms, female genitals are lurid in color, vagrant in contour, and architecturally incoherent. Male genitals, on the other hand, though they risk ludicrousness by their rubbery indecisiveness (a Sylvia Plath heroine memorably thinks of 'turkey neck and turkey gizzards'), have a rational mathematical design, a syntax. This is no absolute

---

[*] 'The Analytic Conception on the Psycho-Neuroses' (1908), in *Further Contributions to the Theory and Technique of Psycho-analysis*, ed. John Rickman, trans. Jane Isabel Suttie et al. (New York, 1926), 25.

virtue, however, since it may tend to confirm the male in his abundant misperceptions of reality. Aesthetics stop where sex begins. G. Wilson Knight declares, 'All physical love is, in its way, a victory over physical secrecies and physical repulsions.'* Sex is sloppy and untidy, a return to what Freud calls the infant's polymorphous perversity, a zestful rolling around in every body fluid. St Augustine says, 'We are born between feces and urine.' This misogynistic view of the infant's sin-stained emergence from the birth canal is close to the chthonian truth. But excretion, through which nature for once acts upon the sexes equally, can be saved by comedy, as we see in Aristophanes, Rabelais, Pope, and Joyce. Excretion has found a place in high culture. Menstruation and childbirth are too barbaric for comedy. Their ugliness has produced the giant displacement of women's historical status as sex object, whose beauty is endlessly discussed and modified. Woman's beauty is a compromise with her dangerous archetypal allure. It gives the eye the comforting illusion of intellectual control over nature.

My explanation for the male domination of art, science, and politics, an indisputable fact of history, is based on an analogy between sexual physiology and aesthetics. I will argue that all cultural achievement is a projection, a swerve into Apollonian transcendance, and that men are anatomically destined to be projectors. But as with Oedipus, destiny may be a curse.

How we know the world and how it knows us are underlain by shadow patterns of sexual biography and sexual geography. What breaks into consciousness is shaped in advance by the daemonism of the senses. Mind is a captive of the body. Perfect

* *Lord Byron's Marriage* (London, 1957), 261.

objectivity does not exist. Every thought bears some emotional burden. Had we time or energy to pursue it, each random choice, from the color of a toothbrush to a decision over a menu, could be made to yield its secret meaning in the inner drama of our lives. But in exhaustion, we shut out this psychic supersaturation. The realm of number, the crystalline mathematic of Apollonian purity, was invented early on by western man as a refuge from the soggy emotionalism and bristling disorder of woman and nature. Women who excel in mathematics do so in a system devised by men for the mastery of nature. Number is the most imposing and least creaturely of pacifiers, man's yearning hope for objectivity. It is to number that he – and now she – withdraws to escape from the chthonian mire of love, hate, and family romance.

Even now, it is usually men rather than women who claim logic's superiority to emotion. This they comically tend to do at moments of maximum emotional chaos, which they may have incited and are helpless to stem. Male artists and actors have a cultural function in keeping the line of emotion open from the female to male realms. Every man harbors an inner female territory ruled by his mother, from whom he can never entirely break free. Since Romanticism, art and the study of art have become vehicles for exploring the west's repressed emotional life, though one would never know it from half the deadening scholarship that has sprung up around them. Poetry is the connecting link between body and mind. Every idea in poetry is grounded in emotion. Every word is a palpation of the body. The multiplicity of interpretation surrounding a poem mirrors the stormy uncontrollability of emotion, where nature works her will. Emotion *is* chaos. Every benign emotion has a flip side of negativity. Thus the flight from emotion to number is another crucial strategy of the Apollonian west in its long struggle with Dionysus.

Emotion is passion, a continuum of eroticism and aggression. Love and hate are not opposites: there is only more passion and less passion, a difference of quantity and not of kind. To live in love and peace is one of the outstanding contradictions that Christianity has imposed on its followers, an ideal impossible and unnatural. Since Romanticism, artists and intellectuals have complained about the church's sex rules, but these are just one small part of the Christian war with pagan nature. Only a saint could sustain the Christian code of love. And saints are ruthless in their exclusions: they must shut out an enormous amount of reality, the reality of sexual personae and the reality of nature. Love for all means coldness to something or someone. Even Jesus, let us recall, was unnecessarily rude to his mother at Cana.

The chthonian superflux of emotion is a male problem. A man must do battle with that enormity, which resides in woman and nature. He can attain selfhood only by beating back the daemonic cloud that would swallow him up: mother-love, which we may just as well call mother-hate. Mother-love, mother-hate, for her or from her, one huge conglomerate of natural power. Political equality for women will make very little difference in this emotional turmoil that is going on above and below politics, outside the scheme of social life. Not until all babies are born from glass jars will the combat cease between mother and son. But in a totalitarian future that has removed procreation from woman's hands, there will also be no affect and no art. Men will be machines, without pain but also without pleasure. Imagination has a price, which we are paying every day. There is no escape from the biologic chains that bind us.

What has nature given man to defend himself against woman? 27

Here we come to the source of man's cultural achievements, which follow so directly from his singular anatomy. Our lives as physical beings give rise to basic metaphors of apprehension, which vary greatly between the sexes. Here there can be no equality. Man is sexually compartmentalized. Genitally, he is condemned to a perpetual pattern of linearity, focus, aim, directedness. He must learn to aim. Without aim, urination and ejaculation end in infantile soiling of self or surroundings. Woman's eroticism is diffused throughout her body. Her desire for foreplay remains a notorious area of miscommunication between the sexes. Man's genital concentration is a reduction but also an intensification. He is a victim of unruly ups and downs. Male sexuality is inherently manic-depressive. Estrogen tranquilizes, but androgen agitates. Men are in a constant state of sexual anxiety, living on the pins and needles of their hormones. In sex as in life they are driven *beyond* – beyond the self, beyond the body. Even in the womb this rule applies. Every fetus becomes female unless it is steeped in male hormone, produced by a signal from the testes. Before birth, therefore, a male is already beyond the female. But to be beyond is to be exiled from the center of life. Men know they are sexual exiles. They wander the earth seeking satisfaction, craving and despising, never content. There is nothing in that anguished motion for women to envy.

The male genital metaphor is concentration and projection. Nature gives concentration to man to help him overcome his fear. Man approaches woman in bursts of spasmodic concentration. This gives him the delusion of temporary control of the archetypal mysteries that brought him forth. It gives him the courage to return. Sex is metaphysical for men, as it is not for women. Women have no problem to solve by sex. Physically and psychologically, they are serenely self-contained. They may choose to achieve, but they do not need it. They are not thrust into the beyond by their own fractious bodies. But men are out of balance. They must quest, pursue, court, or seize. Pigeons on the grass, alas: in such parkside rituals we may savor the comic pathos of sex. How often one spots a male pigeon making desperate, self-inflating sallies toward the female, as again and again she turns her back on him and nonchalantly marches away. But by concentration and insistence he may carry the day. Nature has blessed him with obliviousness to his own absurdity. His purposiveness is both a gift and a burden. In human beings, sexual concentration is the male's instrument for gathering together and forcibly fixing the dangerous chthonian superflux of emotion and energy that I identify with woman and nature. In sex, man is driven into the very abyss which he flees. He makes a voyage to nonbeing and back.

Through concentration to projection into the beyond. The male projection of erection and ejaculation is the paradigm for all cultural projection and conceptualization – from art and philosophy to fantasy, hallucination, and obsession. Women have conceptualized less in history not because men have kept them from doing so but because women do not need to conceptualize in order to exist. I leave open the question of brain differences. Conceptualization and sexual mania may issue from the same part of the male brain. Fetishism, for instance, a practice which like most of the sex perversions is confined to men, is clearly a conceptualizing or symbol-making activity. Man's vastly greater commercial patronage of pornography is analogous.

An erection is *a thought* and the orgasm an act of imagination. The male has to will his sexual authority before the woman who is a shadow of his mother and of all women. Failure and humiliation constantly wait in the wings. No woman has to   29 prove herself a woman in the grim way a man has to prove himself a man. He must perform, or the show does not go on. Social convention is irrelevant. A flop is a flop. Ironically, sexual success always ends in sagging fortunes anyhow. Every male projection is transient and must be anxiously, endlessly renewed. Men enter in triumph but withdraw in decrepitude. The sex act cruelly mimics history's decline and fall. Male bonding is a self-preservation society, collegial reaffirmation through larger, fabricated frames of reference. Culture is man's iron reinforcement of his ever-imperiled private projections.

Concentration and projection are remarkably demonstrated by urination, one of male anatomy's most efficient compartmentalizations. Freud thinks primitive man preened himself on his ability to put out a fire with a stream of urine. A strange thing to be proud of but certainly beyond the scope of woman, who would scorch her hams in the process. Male urination really *is* a kind of accomplishment, an arc of transcendance. A woman merely waters the ground she stands on. Male urination is a form of commentary. It can be friendly when shared but is often aggressive, as in the defacement of public monuments by Sixties rock stars. To piss on is to criticize. John Wayne urinated on the shoes of a grouchy director in full view of cast and crew. This is one genre of self-expression women will never master. A male dog marking every bush on the block is a graffiti artist, leaving his rude signature with each lift of the leg. Women, like female dogs, are earthbound squatters. There is no projection beyond the boundaries of the self. Space is claimed by being sat on, squatter's rights.

The cumbersome, solipsistic character of female physiology is tediously evident at sports events and rock concerts, where fifty women wait in line for admission to the sequestered cells of the toilet. Meanwhile, their male friends zip in and out (in every sense) and stand around looking at their watches and rolling their eyes. Freud's notion of penis envy proves too true when the pubcrawling male cheerily relieves himself in midnight alleyways, to the vexation of his bursting female companions. This compart-mentalization or isolation of male genitality has its dark side, however. It can lead to a dissociation of sex and emotion, to temptation, promiscuity, and disease. The modern male homo-sexual, for example, has sought ecstasy in the squalor of public toilets, for women perhaps the least erotic place on earth.

Man's metaphors of concentration and projection are echoes of both body and mind. Without them, he would be helpless before woman's power. Without them, woman would long ago have absorbed all of creation into herself. There would be no culture, no system, no pyramiding of one hierarchy upon another. Earth-cult must lose to sky-cult, if mind is ever to break free from matter. Ironically, the more modern woman thinks with Apollonian clarity, the more she participates in the historical negation of her sex. Political equality for women, desirable and necessary as it is, is not going to remedy the radical disjunction between the sexes that begins and ends in the body. The sexes will always be jolted by violent shocks of attraction and repulsion.

Androgyny, which some feminists promote as a pacifist blue-print for sexual utopia, belongs to the contemplative rather than active life. It is the ancient prerogative of priests, shamans, and artists. Feminists have politicized it as a weapon against the masculine principle. Redefined, it now means men must be like women and women can be whatever they like. Androgyny is a cancellation of male concentration and projection. Prescriptions for the future by bourgeois academics and writers carry their own bias. The reform of a college English department cuts no ice down at the corner garage. Male concentration and projection are visible everywhere in the aggressive energy of the streets. Fortunately, male homosexuals of every social class have preserved the cult of the masculine, which will therefore never lose its aesthetic legitimacy. Major peaks of western culture have been accompanied by a high incidence of male homosexuality – in classical Athens and Renaissance Florence and London. Male concentration and projection are self-enhancing, leading to supreme achievements of Apollonian conceptualization.

If sexual physiology provides the pattern for our experience of the world, what is woman's basic metaphor? It is mystery, *the hidden*. Karen Horney speaks of a girl's inability to see her genitals and a boy's ability to see his as the source of 'the greater subjectivity of women as compared with the greater objectivity of men.'* To rephrase this with my different emphasis: men's delusional certitude that objectivity is possible is based on the visibility of their genitals. Second, this certitude is a defensive swerve from the anxiety-inducing invisibility of the womb. Women tend to be more realistic and less obsessional because of their toleration for ambiguity, which they learn from their inability to learn about their own bodies. Women accept limited knowledge as their natural condition, a great human truth that a man may take a lifetime to reach.

The female body's unbearable hiddenness applies to all aspects of men's dealings with women. What does it look like in there? Did she have an orgasm? Is it really my child? Who was my real father? Mystery shrouds woman's sexuality. This mystery is the

* 'On the Genesis of the Castration Complex in Women', *International Journal of Psychoanalysis* 5 (1924): 53.

main reason for the imprisonment man has imposed on women. Only by confining his wife in a locked harem guarded by eunuchs could he be certain that her son was also his. Man's genital visibility is a source of his scientific desire for external testing, validation, proof. By this method he hopes to solve the ultimate mystery story, his chthonian birth. Woman is veiled. Violent tearing of this veil may be a motive in gang-rapes and rape-murders, particularly ritualistic disembowellings of the Jack the Ripper kind. The Ripper's public nailing up of his victim's uterus is exactly paralleled in tribal ritual of South African Bushmen. Sex crimes are always male, never female, because such crimes are conceptualizing assaults on the unreachable omnipotence of woman and nature. Every woman's body contains a cell of archaic night, where all knowing must stop. This is the profound meaning behind striptease, a sacred dance of pagan origins which, like prostitution, Christianity has never been able to stamp out. Erotic dancing by males cannot be comparable, for a nude woman carries off the stage a final concealment, that chthonian darkness from which we come.

Woman's body is a secret, sacred space. It is a *temenos* or ritual precinct, a Greek word I adopt for the discussion of art. In the marked-off space of woman's body, nature operates at its darkest and most mechanical. Every woman is a priestess guarding the temenos of daemonic mysteries. Virginity is categorically different for the sexes. A boy becoming a man quests for experience. The penis is like eye or hand, an extension of self reaching outward. But a girl is a sealed vessel that must be broken into by force. The female body is the prototype of all sacred spaces from cave shrine to temple and church. The womb is the veiled Holy of Holies, a great problem, as we shall see, for sexual polemicists like William Blake who seek to abolish guilt 33 and covertness in sex. The taboo on woman's body is the taboo that always hovers over the place of magic. Woman is literally the occult, which means 'the hidden'. These uncanny meanings cannot be changed, only suppressed, until they break into cultural consciousness again. Political equality will succeed only in political terms. It is helpless against the archetypal. Kill the imagination, lobotomize the brain, castrate and operate: then the sexes will be the same. Until then, we must live and dream in the daemonic turbulence of nature.

Everything sacred and inviolable provokes profanation and violation. Every crime that *can* be committed *will* be. Rape is a mode of natural aggression that can be controlled only by the social contract. Modern feminism's most naive formulation is its assertion that rape is a crime of violence but not of sex, that it is merely power masquerading as sex. But sex *is* power, and all power is inherently aggressive. Rape is male power fighting female power. It is no more to be excused than is murder or any other assault on another's civil rights. Society is woman's protection against rape, not, as some feminists absurdly maintain, the cause of rape. Rape is the sexual expression of the will-to-power, which nature plants in all of us and which civilization rose to contain. Therefore the rapist is a man with too little socialization rather than too much. Worldwide evidence is overwhelming that whenever social controls are weakened, as in war or mob rule, even civilized men behave in uncivilized ways, among which is the barbarity of rape.

The latent metaphors of the body guarantee the survival of rape, which is a development in degree of intensity alone of the basic movements of sex. A girl's loss of virginity is always in some sense a violation of sanctity, an invasion of her integrity and identity. Defloration *is* destruction. But nature creates by violence and destruction. The commonest violence in the world is childbirth, with its appalling pain and gore. Nature gives males infusions of hormones for dominance in order to hurl them against the paralyzing mystery of woman, from whom they would otherwise shrink. Her power as mistress of birth is already too extreme. Lust and aggression are fused in male hormones. Anyone who doubts this has probably never spent much time around horses. Stallions are so dangerous they must be caged in barred stalls; once gelded, they are docile enough to serve as children's mounts. The hormonal disparity in humans is not so gross, but it is grosser than Rousseauists like to think. The more testosterone, the more elevated the libido. The more dominant the male, the more frequent his contributions to the genetic pool. Even on the microscopic level, male fertility is a function not only of number of sperm but of their motility, that is, their restless movement, which increases the chance of conception. Sperm are miniature assault troops, and the ovum is a solitary citadel that must be breached. Weak or passive sperm just sit there like dead ducks. Nature rewards energy and aggression.

Profanation and violation are part of the perversity of sex, which never will conform to liberal theories of benevolence. Every model of morally or politically correct sexual behavior *will be subverted*, by nature's daemonic law. Every hour of every day, some horror is being committed somewhere. Feminism, arguing from the milder woman's view, completely misses the blood-lust in rape, the joy of violation and destruction. An aesthetics and erotics of profanation – evil for the sake of evil, the sharpening of the senses by cruelty and torture – have been documented in Sade, Baudelaire, and Huysmans. Women may be less prone to such fantasies because they physically lack the equipment for 35 sexual violence. They do not know the temptation of forcibly invading the sanctuary of another body.

Our knowledge of these fantasies is expanded by pornography, which is why pornography should be tolerated, though its public display may reasonably be restricted. The imagination cannot and must not be policed. Pornography shows us nature's daemonic heart, those eternal forces at work beneath and beyond social convention. Pornography cannot be separated from art; the two interpenetrate each other, far more than humanistic criticism has admitted. Geoffrey Hartman rightly says, 'Great art is always flanked by its dark sisters, blasphemy and pornography.'* *Hamlet* itself, the cardinal western work, is full of lewdness. Criminals through history, from Nero and Caligula to Gilles de Rais and the Nazi commandants, have never needed pornography to stimulate their exquisite, gruesome inventiveness. The diabolic human mind is quite enough.

Happy are those periods when marriage and religion are strong. System and order shelter us against sex and nature. Unfortunately, we live in a time when the chaos of sex has broken into the open. G. Wilson Knight remarks, 'Christianity came originally as a tearing down of taboos in the name of a sacred humanity; but the Church it gave rise to has never yet succeeded in Christianizing the pagan evil magic of sex.'† Historiography's most glaring error has been its assertion that Judeo-Christianity defeated paganism. Paganism has survived in the thousand forms of sex, art, and now the modern media. Christianity has made adjustment after adjustment, ingeniously absorbing its opposition

* *Beyond Formalism: Literary Essays 1958–1970* (New Haven, 1970), 23.
† *Atlantic Crossing* (London, 1936), 111.

(as during the Italian Renaissance) and diluting its dogma to change with changing times. But a critical point has been reached. With the rebirth of the gods in the massive idolatries of popular culture, with the eruption of sex and violence into every corner of the ubiquitous mass media, Judeo-Christianity is facing its most serious challenge since Europe's confrontation with Islam in the Middle Ages. The latent paganism of western culture has burst forth again in all its daemonic vitality.

Paganism never was the unbridled sexual licentiousness portrayed by missionaries of the young, embattled Christianity. Singling out as typical of paganism the orgies of bored late Roman aristocrats would be as unfair as singling out as typical of Christianity the sins of renegade priests or the Vatican revels of Pope Alexander VI. True orgy was a ceremony of the chthonian mother-cults in which there were both sex and bloodshed. Paganism recognized, honored, and feared nature's daemonism, and it limited sexual expression by ritual formulae. Christianity was a development of Dionysian mystery religion which paradoxically tried to suppress nature in favor of a transcendental other world. The sole contact with nature that Christianity permitted its followers was sex sanctified by marriage. Chthonian nature, embodied in great goddess figures, was Christianity's most formidable opponent. Christianity works best when revered institutions like monasticism or universal marriage channel sexual energy in positive directions. Western civilization has profited enormously from the sublimation Christianity forced on sex. Christianity works least when sex is constantly stimulated from other directions, as it is now. No transcendental religion can compete with the spectacular pagan nearness and concreteness of the carnal-red media. Our eyes and ears are drowned in a sensual torrent.

The pagan ritual identity of sex and violence is mass media's chief check to the complacent Rousseauism of modern humanists. The commercial media, responding directly to popular patronage, sidestep the liberal censors who have enjoyed such long control over book culture. In film, popular music, and commercials, we contemplate all the daemonic myths and sexual stereotypes of paganism that reform movements from Christianity to feminism have never been able to eradicate. The sexes are eternally at war. There is an element of attack, of search-and-destroy in male sex, in which there will always be a potential for rape. There is an element of entrapment in female sex, a subliminal manipulation leading to physical and emotional infantilization of the male. Freud notes, apropos of his theory of the primal scene, that a child overhearing his parents having sex thinks male is wounding female and that the woman's cries of pleasure are cries of pain. Most men merely grunt, at best. But woman's strange sexual cries come directly from the chthonian. She is a Maenad about to rend her victim. Sex is an uncanny moment of ritual and incantation, in which we hear woman's barbaric ululation of triumph of the will. One domination dissolves into another. The dominated becomes the dominator.

Every menstruating or childbearing woman is a pagan and primitive cast back to those distant ocean shores from which we have never fully evolved. On the streets of every city, prostitutes, the world's oldest profession, stand as a rebuke to sexual morality. They are the daemonic face of nature, initiates of pagan mysteries. Prostitution is not just a service industry, mopping up the overflow of male demand, which always exceeds female supply. Prostitution testifies to the amoral power struggle of sex, which religion has never been able to stop. Prostitutes, pornographers, and their patrons are marauders in the forest of archaic night.

That nature acts upon the sexes differently is proved by the test case of modern male and female homosexuality, illustrating how the sexes function separately outside social convention. The result, according to statistics of sexual frequency: male satyriasis and female nesting. The male homosexual has sex more often than his heterosexual counterpart; the female homosexual less often than hers, a radical polarization of the sexes along a single continuum of shared sexual nonconformity. Male aggression and lust are the energizing factors in culture. They are men's tools of survival in the pagan vastness of female nature.

The old 'double standard' gave men a sexual liberty denied to women. Marxist feminists reduce the historical cult of woman's virginity to her property value, her worth on the male marriage market. I would argue instead that there was and is a biologic basis to the double standard. The first medical reports on the disease killing male homosexuals indicated men most at risk were those with a thousand partners over their lifetime. Incredulity. Who could such people be? Why, it turned out, everyone one knew. Serious, kind, literate men, not bums or thugs. What an abyss divides the sexes! Let us abandon the pretense of sexual sameness and admit the terrible duality of gender.

Male sex is quest romance, exploration and speculation. Promiscuity in men may cheapen love but sharpen thought. Promiscuity in women is illness, a leakage of identity. The promiscuous woman is self-contaminated and incapable of clear ideas. She has ruptured the ritual integrity of her body. It is in nature's best interests to goad dominant males into indiscriminate spreading of their seed. But nature also profits from female purity. Even in the liberated or lesbian woman there is some biologic restraint whispering: keep the birth canal clean. In judiciously withholding herself, woman protects an invisible fetus. Perhaps this is the 39 reason for the archetypal horror (rather than socialized fear) that many otherwise bold women have of spiders and other rapidly crawling insects. Women hold themselves in reserve because the female body is a reservoir, a virgin patch of still, pooled water where the fetus comes to term. Male chase and female flight are not just a social game. The double standard may be one of nature's organic laws.

The quest romance of male sex is a war between identity and annihilation. An erection is a hope for objectivity, for power to act as a free agent. But at the climax of his success, woman is pulling the male back to her bosom, drinking and quelling his energy. Freud says, 'Man fears that his strength will be taken from him by woman, dreads becoming infected with her femininity and then proving himself a weakling.'* Masculinity must fight off effeminacy day by day. Woman and nature stand ever ready to reduce the male to boy and infant.

The operations of sex are convulsive, from intercourse through menstruation and childbirth: tension and distention, spasm, contraction, expulsion, relief. The body is wrenched in serpentine swelling and sloughing. Sex is not the pleasure principle but the Dionysian bondage of pleasure-pain. So much is a matter of *overcoming resistance*, in the body or the beloved, that rape will always be a present danger. Male sex is repetition-compulsion: whatever a man writes in the commentary of his phallic projections must be rewritten again and again. Sexual man is the magician sawing the lady in half, yet the serpent head and tail always live and rejoin. Projection is a male curse: forever to need something or someone to make oneself complete. This is one of

* *Sexuality and the Psychology of Love*, ed. Philip Rieff (New York, 1963), 76.

the sources of art and the secret of its historical domination by males. The artist is the closest man has come to imitating woman's superb self-containment. But the artist needs his art, his projection. The blocked artist, like Leonardo, suffers tortures of the damned. The most famous painting in the world, the *Mona Lisa*, records woman's self-satisfied apartness, her ambiguous mocking smile at the vanity and despair of her many sons.

Everything great in western culture has come from the quarrel with nature. The west and not the east has seen the frightful brutality of natural process, the insult to mind in the heavy blind rolling and milling of matter. In loss of self we would find not love or God but primeval squalor. This revelation has historically fallen upon the western male, who is pulled by tidal rhythms back to the oceanic mother. It is to his resentment of this daemonic undertow that we owe the grand constructions of our culture. Apollonianism, cold and absolute, is the west's sublime refusal. The Apollonian is a male line drawn against the dehumanizing magnitude of female nature.

Everything is melting in nature. We think we see objects, but our eyes are slow and partial. Nature is blooming and withering in long puffy respirations, rising and falling in oceanic wave-motion. A mind that opened itself fully to nature without sentimental preconception would be glutted by nature's coarse materialism, its relentless superfluity. An apple tree laden with fruit: how peaceful, how picturesque. But remove the rosy filter of humanism from our gaze and look again. See nature spurning and frothing, its mad spermatic bubbles endlessly spilling out and smashing in that inhuman round of waste, rot, and carnage. From the jammed glassy cells of sea roe to the feathery spores poured into the air from bursting green pods, nature is a festering hornet's nest of aggression and overkill. This is the chthonian black magic with which we are infected as sexual beings; this is the daemonic identity that Christianity so inadequately defines as original sin and thinks it can cleanse us of. Procreative woman is the most troublesome obstacle to Christianity's claim to catholicity, testified by its wishful doctrines of Immaculate Conception and Virgin Birth. The procreativeness of chthonian nature is an obstacle to all of western metaphysics and to each man in his quest for identity against his mother. Nature is the seething excess of being.

The most effective weapon against the flux of nature is art. Religion, ritual, and art began as one, and a religious or metaphysical element is still present in all art. Art, no matter how minimalist, is never simply design. It is always a ritualistic reordering of reality. The enterprise of art, in a stable collective era or an unsettled individualistic one, is inspired by anxiety. Every subject localized and honored by art is endangered by its opposite. Art is a *shutting in* in order to *shut out*. Art is a ritualistic binding of the perpetual motion machine that is nature. The first artist was a tribal priest casting a spell, fixing nature's daemonic energy in a moment of perceptual stillness. Fixation is at the heart of art, fixation as stasis and fixation as obsession. The modern artist who merely draws a line across a page is still trying to tame some uncontrollable aspect of reality. Art is spellbinding. Art fixes the audience in its seat, stops the feet before a painting, fixes a book in the hand. Contemplation is a magic act.

Art is order. But order is not necessarily just, kind, or beautiful. Order may be arbitrary, harsh, and cruel. Art has nothing to do with morality. Moral themes may be present, but they are incidental, simply grounding an art work in a particular time and place. Before the Enlightenment, religious art was

42

hieratic and ceremonial. After the Enlightenment, art had to create its own world, in which a new ritual of artistic formalism replaced religious universals. Eighteenth-century Augustan literature demonstrates it is the order in morality rather than the morality in order that attracts the artist. Only utopian liberals could be surprised that the Nazis were art connoisseurs. Particularly in modern times, when high art has been shoved to the periphery of culture, is it evident that art is aggressive and compulsive. The artist makes art not to save humankind but to save himself. Every benevolent remark by an artist is a fog to cover his tracks, the bloody trail of his assault against reality and others.

Art is a temenos, a sacred place. It is ritually clean, a swept floor, the threshing floor that was the first site of theater. Whatever enters this space is transformed. From the bison of cave painting to Hollywood movie stars, represented beings enter a cultic other life from which they may never emerge. They are spellbound. Art is sacrificial, turning its inherent aggression against both artist and representation. Nietzsche says, 'Almost everything we call "higher culture" is based on the spiritualization of *cruelty*.'* Literature's endless murders and disasters are there for contemplative pleasure, not moral lesson. Their status as fiction, removed into a sacred precinct, intensifies our pleasure by guaranteeing that contemplation cannot turn into action. No lunge by a compassionate spectator can avert the cool inevitability of that hieratic ceremony, ritually replayed through time. The blood that is shed will always be shed. Ritual in church or theater is amoral fixation, dispelling anxiety by formalizing and freezing emotion. The ritual of art is the cruel law of pain made pleasure.

* *Beyond Good and Evil*, trans. Walter Kaufmann (New York, 1966), 158.

Art makes *things*. There are, I said, no objects in nature, only the gruelling erosion of natural force, flecking, dilapidating, grinding down, reducing all matter to fluid, the thick primal soup from which new forms bob, gasping for life. Dionysus was identified with liquids – blood, sap, milk, wine. The Dionysian is nature's chthonian fluidity. Apollo, on the other hand, gives form and shape, marking off one being from another. All artifacts are Apollonian. Melting and union are Dionysian; separation and individuation, Apollonian. Every boy who leaves his mother to become a man is turning the Apollonian against the Dionysian. Every artist who is compelled toward art, who needs to make words or pictures as others need to breathe, is using the Apollonian to defeat chthonian nature. In sex, men must mediate between Apollo and Dionysus. Sexually, woman can remain oblique, opaque, taking pleasure without tumult or conflict. Woman is a temenos of her own dark mysteries. Genitally, man has a little thing that he must keep dipping in Dionysian dissolution – a risky business! Thing-making, thing-preserving is central to male experience. Man is a fetishist. Without his fetish, woman will just gobble him up again.

Hence the male domination of art and science. Man's focus, directedness, concentration, and projection, which I identified with urination and ejaculation, are his tools of sexual survival, but they have never given him a final victory. The anxiety in sexual experience remains as strong as ever. This man attempts to correct by the cult of female beauty. He is erotically fixated on woman's 'shapeliness', those spongy maternal fat deposits of breast, hip, and buttock which are ironically the wateriest and least stable parts of her anatomy Woman's billowy body reflects the surging sea of chthonian nature. By focusing on the shapely, by making woman a sex-object, man has struggled to fix and stabilize nature's dreadful flux. Objectification is conceptualization, the highest human faculty. Turning people into sex objects is one of the specialties of our species. It will never disappear, since it is intertwined with the art-impulse and may be identical to it. A sex-object is ritual form imposed on nature. It is a totem of our perverse imagination.

Apollonian thing-making is the main line of western civilization, extending from ancient Egypt to the present. Every attempt to repress this aspect of our culture has ultimately been defeated. First Judaism, then Christianity turned against pagan idol-making. But Christianity, with wider impact than Judaism, became the most art-laden, art-dominated religion in the world. Imagination always remedies the defects of religion. The hardest object of Apollonian thing-making is western personality, the glamorous, striving, separatist ego that entered literature in the *Iliad* but, I will show, first appeared in art in Old Kingdom Egypt.

Christianity, wiping out paganism's secular glamours, tried to make spirituality primary. But as an embattled sect, it ended by reinforcing the west's absolutist ego-structure. The hero of the medieval Church militant, the knight in shining armour, is the most perfect Apollonian *thing* in world history. Art books need to be rewritten: there is a direct line from Greek and Roman sculpture through medieval armour to the Renaissance revival of classicism. Arms and armour are not handicrafts but art. They carry the symbolic weight of western personality. Armour is the pagan continuity in medieval Christianity. After the Renaissance released the sensual, idolatrous art-making of classicism, the pagan line has continued in brazen force to today. The idea that the western tradition collapsed after World War One is one of 45 the myopic little sulks of liberalism. I will argue that high culture made itself obsolete through modernism's neurotic nihilism and that popular culture is the great heir of the western past. Cinema is the supreme Apollonian genre, thing-making and thing-made, a machine of the gods.

Man, the sexual conceptualizer and projector, has ruled art because art is his Apollonian response toward and away from woman. A sex object is something to aim at. The eye is Apollo's arrow following the arc of transcendance I saw in male urination and ejaculation. The western eye is a projectile into the *beyond*, that wilderness of the male condition. By no coincidence, Europe first made firearms for gunpowder, which China had invented centuries earlier but found little use for. Phallic aggression and projection are intrinsic to western conceptualization. Arrow, eye, gun, cinema: the blazing lightbeam of the movie projector is our modern path of Apollonian transcendance. Cinema is the culmination of the obsessive, mechanistic male drive in western culture. The movie projector is an Apollonian straightshooter, demonstrating the link between aggression and art. Every pictorial framing is a ritual limitation, a barred precinct. The rectangular movie screen is clearly patterned on the post-Renaissance framed painting. But all conceptualization is a framing.

The history of costume belongs to art history but is too often regarded as a journalistic lady's adjunct to scholarship. There is nothing trivial about fashion. Standards of beauty are conceptualizations projected by each culture. They tell us everything. Women have been the most victimized by fashion's ever-turning wheel, binding their feet or bosom to phantom commands. But fashion is not just one more political oppression to add to the feminist litany. Standards of beauty, created by men but usually consented to by women, ritually limit women's archetypal sexual allure. Fashion is an externalization of woman's daemonic invisibility, her genital mystery. It brings before man's Apollonian eye what that eye can never see. Beauty is an Apollonian freeze-frame: it halts and condenses the flux and indeterminacy of nature. It allows man to act by enhancing the desirability of what he fears.

The power of the eye in western culture has not been fully appreciated or analyzed. The Asian abases the eyes and transfers value into a mystic third eye, marked by the red dot on the Hindu forehead. Personality is inauthentic in the east, which identifies self with group. Eastern meditation rejects historical time. We have a parallel religious tradition: the paradoxical axioms of eastern and western mystics and poets are often indistinguishable. Buddhism and Christianity agree in seeing the material world as *samsara*, the veil of illusion. But the west has another tradition, the pagan, culminating in cinema. The west makes personality and history numinous objects of contemplation. Western personality is a work of art, and history is its stage. The twentieth century is not the Age of Anxiety but the Age of Hollywood. The pagan cult of personality has reawakened and dominates all art, all thought. It is morally empty but ritually profound. We worship it by the power of the western eye. Movie screen and television screen are its sacred precincts.

Western culture has a roving eye. Male sex is hunting and scanning: boys hang yelping from honking cars, acting like jerks over strolling girls; men lunching on girders go through the primitive book of wolf whistles and animal clucks. Everywhere, the beautiful woman is scrutinized and harassed. She is the ultimate symbol of human desire. The feminine is that-which-is-sought; it recedes beyond our grasp. Hence there is always a feminine element in the beautiful young man of male 47 homosexuality. The feminine is the ever-elusive, a silver shimmer on the horizon. We follow this image with longing eyes: maybe this one, maybe this time. The pursuit of sex may conceal a dream of being freed from sex. Sex, knowledge, and power are deeply tangled; we cannot get one without the others. Islam is wise to drape women in black, for the eye is the avenue of eros. Western culture's hard, defined personalities suffer from inflammation of the eye. They are so numerous that they have never been catalogued, except in our magnificent portrait art. Western sexual personae are nodes of power, but they have made a torment of eroticism. From this torment has come our grand tradition of literature and art. Unfortunately, there is no way to separate the whistling ass on his girder from the rapt visionary at his easel. In accepting the gifts of culture, women may have to take the worm with the apple.

Judeo-Christianity has failed to control the pagan western eye. Our thought processes were formed in Greece and inherited by Rome, whose language remains the official voice of the Catholic church. Intellectual inquiry and logic are pagan. Every inquiry is preceded by a roving eye; and once the eye begins to rove, it cannot be morally controlled. Judaism, due to its fear of the eye, put a taboo on visual representation. Judaism is based on word rather than image. Christianity followed suit, until it drifted into pictorialism to appeal to the pagan masses. Protestantism began as an iconoclasm, a breaking of the images of the corrupt Roman church. The pure Protestant style is a bare white church with plain windows. Italian Catholicism, I am happy to say, retains the most florid pictorialism, the bequest of a pagan past that was never lost.

Paganism is eye-intense. It is based on cultic exhibitionism, in which sex and sadomasochism are joined. The ancient chthonian mysteries have never disappeared from the Italian church. Waxed saints' corpses under glass. Tattered armbones in gold reliquaries. Half-nude St Sebastian pierced by arrows. St Lucy holding her eyeballs out on a platter. Blood, torture, ecstasy, and tears. Its lurid sensationalism makes Italian Catholicism the emotionally most complete cosmology in religious history. Italy added pagan sex and violence to the ascetic Palestinian creed. And so to Hollywood, the modern Rome: it is pagan sex and violence that have flowered so vividly in our mass media. The camera has unbound daemonic western imagination. Cinema is *sexual showing*, a pagan flaunting. Plot and dialogue are obsolete word-baggage. Cinema, the most eye-intense of genres, has restored pagan antiquity's cultic exhibitionism. Spectacle is a pagan cult of the eye.

There is no such thing as 'mere' image. Western culture is built on perceptual relations. From the soaring god-projections of ancient sky-cult to the celebrity-inflating machinery of American commercial promotion, western identity has organized itself around charismatic sexual personae of hierarchic command. Every god is an idol, literally an 'image' (Latin *idolum* from Greek *eidolon*). Image is implied visibility. The visual is sorely undervalued in modern scholarship. Art history has attained only a fraction of the conceptual sophistication of literary criticism. And literature and art remain unmeshed. Drunk with self-love, criticism has hugely overestimated the centrality of language to western culture. It has failed to see the electrifying sign language of images.

The war between Judeo-Christianity and paganism is still being waged in the latest ideologies of the university. Freud, as a Jew, may have been biased in favor of the word. In my opinion, Freudian theory overstates the linguistic character of the 49 unconscious and slights the gorgeously cinematic pictorialism of the dream life. Furthermore, arguments by the French about the rationalist limitations of their own culture have been illegitimately transferred to England and America, with poor results. The English language was created by poets, a five-hundred-year enterprise of emotion and metaphor, the richest internal dialogue in world literature. French rhetorical models are too narrow for the English tradition. Most pernicious of French imports is the notion that there is no person behind a text. Is there anything *more* affected, aggressive, and relentlessly concrete than a Parisian intellectual behind his/her turgid text? The Parisian is a provincial when he pretends to speak for the universe. Behind every book is a certain person with a certain history. I can never know too much about that person and that history. Personality is western reality. It is a visible condensation of sex and psyche outside the realm of word. We know it by Apollonian vision, the pagan cinema of western perception. Let us not steal from the eye to give to the ear.

Word-worship has made it difficult for scholarship to deal with the radical cultural change of our era of mass media. Academics are constantly fighting a rearguard action. Traditional genre-criticism is moribund. The humanities must abandon their insular fiefdoms and begin thinking in terms of *imagination*, a power that crosses the genres and unites high with popular art, the noble with the sleazy. There is neither decline nor disaster in the triumph of mass media, only a shift from word to image – in other words, a return to western culture's pre-Gutenberg, pre-Protestant pagan pictorialism.

That popular culture reclaims what high culture shuts out is clear in the case of pornography. Pornography is pure pagan imagism. Just as a poem is ritually limited verbal expression, so is pornography ritually limited visual expression of the daemonism of sex and nature. Every shot, every angle in pornography, no matter how silly, twisted, or pasty is yet another attempt to *get the whole picture* of the enormity of chthonian nature. Is pornography art? Yes. Art is contemplation and conceptualization, the ritual exhibitionism of primal mysteries. Art makes order of nature's cyclonic brutality. Art, I said, is full of crimes. The ugliness and violence in pornography reflect the ugliness and violence in nature.

Pornography's male-born explicitness renders visible what is invisible, woman's chthonian internality. It tries to shed Apollonian light on woman's anxiety-provoking darkness. The vulgar contortionism of pornography is the serpentine tangle of Medusan nature. Pornography is human imagination in tense theatrical action; its violations are a protest against the violations of our freedom by nature. The banning of pornography, rightly sought by Judeo-Christianity, would be a victory over the west's stubborn paganism. But pornography cannot be banned, only driven underground, where its illicit charge will be enhanced. Pornography's amoral pictorialism will live forever as a rebuke to the humanistic cult of the redemptive word. Words cannot save the cruel flux of pagan nature.

The western eye makes *things*, idols of Apollonian objectification. Pornography makes many well-meaning people uncomfortable because it isolates the voyeuristic element present in all art, and especially cinema. All the personae of art are sex objects. The emotional response of spectator or reader is inseparable from erotic response. As I said, our lives as physical beings are a Dionysian continuum of pleasure-pain. At every moment we are steeped in the sensory, even in sleep. Emotional arousal is sensual arousal; sensual arousal is sexual arousal. The idea that 51 emotion can be separated from sex is a Christian illusion, one of the most ingenious but finally unworkable strategies in Christianity's ancient campaign against pagan nature. Agape, spiritual love, belongs to eros but has run away from home.

We are voyeurs at the perimeters of art, and there is a sadomasochistic sensuality in our responses to it. Art is a scandal, literally a 'stumbling block', to all moralism, whether on the Christian right or Rousseauist left. Pornography and art are inseparable, because there is voyeurism and voracity in all our sensations as seeing, feeling beings. The fullest exploration of these ideas is Edmund Spenser's Renaissance epic, *The Faerie Queene*. In this poem, which prefigures cinema by its radiant Apollonian projections, the voyeuristic and sadomasochistic latency in art and sex is copiously documented. Western perception is a daemonic theater of ritual surprise. We may not like what we see when we look into the dark mirror of art.

Sex object, art work, personality: western experience is cellular and divisive. It imposes a graph of marked-off spaces on nature's continuity and flow. We have made Apollonian demarcations that function as ritual preserves against nature; hence our complex criminal codes and elaborate erotics of transgression. The weakness in radical critiques of sex and society is that they fail to recognize that sex needs ritual binding to control its daemonism and secondly that society's repressions *increase* sexual pleasure. There is nothing less erotic than a nudist colony. Desire is intensified by ritual limitations. Hence the mask, harness, and chains of sadomasochism.

The western cells of holiness and criminality are a cognitive advance in human history. Our cardinal myths are Faust, who locks himself in his study to read books and crack the code of nature, and Don Juan, who makes a war of pleasure and counts his conquests by Apollonian number. Both are cellular egos, seducers and criminal knowers, in whom sex, thought, and aggression are fused. This cell separated from nature is our brain and eye. Our hard personalities are imagistic projections from the Apollonian higher cortex. Personae are visible ideas. All facial expressions and theatrical postures, present among animal primates, are fleeting shadows of personae. While Japanese decorum limits facial expressions, western art since the Hellenistic era has recorded every permutation of irony, anxiety, flirtation, and menace. The hardness of our personalities and the tension with which they are set off from nature have produced the west's vulnerability to decadence. Tension leads to fatigue and collapse, 'late' phases of history in which sadomasochism flourishes. As I will show, decadence is a *disease of the eye*, a sexual intensification of artistic voyeurism.

The Apollonian *things* of western sex and art reach their economic glorification in capitalism. In the past fifteen years, Marxist approaches to literature have enjoyed increasing vogue. To be conscious of the social context of art seems automatically to entail a leftist orientation. But a theory is possible that is both avant-garde *and* capitalist. Marxism was one of Rousseau's nineteenth-century progeny, energized by faith in the perfectibility of man. Its belief that economic forces are the primary dynamic in history is Romantic naturism in disguise. That is, it sketches a surging wave-motion in the material context of human life but tries to deny the perverse daemonism of that context. Marxism is the bleakest of anxiety-formations against the power of chthonian mothers. Its influence on modern historiography has been excessive. The 'great man' theory of history was not as simplistic as claimed; we have barely recovered from a world war in which this theory was proved evilly true. One man *can* change 53 the course of history, for good or ill. Marxism is a flight from the magic of person and the mystique of hierarchy. It distorts the character of western culture, which is based on charismatic power of person. Marxism can work only in pre-industrial societies of homogeneous populations. Raise the standard of living, and the rainbow riot of individualism will break out. Personality and art, which Marxism fears and censors, rebound from every effort to repress them.

Capitalism, gaudy and greedy, has been inherent in western aesthetics from ancient Egypt on. It is the mysticism and glamour of *things*, which take on a personality of their own. As an economic system, it is in the Darwinian line of Sade, not Rousseau. The capitalist survival of the fittest is already present in the *Iliad*. Western sexual personae clash by day and by night. Homer's gleaming bronze-clad warriors are the Apollonian soup cans that crowd the sunny temples of our supermarkets and compete for our attention on television. The west objectifies persons and personalizes objects. The teeming multiplicity of capitalist products is an Apollonian correction of nature. Brand names are territorial cells of western identity. Our shiny chrome automobiles, like our armies of grocery boxes and cans, are extrapolations of hard, impermeable western personality.

Capitalist products are another version of the art works flooding western culture. The portable framed painting appeared at the birth of modern commerce in the early Renaissance. Capitalism and art have challenged and nourished each other ever since. Capitalist and artist are parallel types: the artist is just as amoral and acquisitive as the capitalist, and just as hostile to competitors. That in the age of the merchant-prince art works are hawked and sold like hot dogs supports my argument but is not central to it. Western culture is animated by a visionary materialism.

Apollonian formalism has stolen from nature to make a romance of *things*, hard, shiny, crass, and willful.

The capitalist distribution network, a complex chain of factory, transport, warehouse, and retail outlet, is one of the greatest male accomplishments in the history of culture. It is a lightning-quick Apollonian circuit of male bonding. One of feminism's irritating reflexes is its fashionable disdain for 'patriarchal society', to which nothing good is ever attributed. But it is patriarchal society that has freed me as a woman. It is capitalism that has given me the leisure to sit at this desk writing this book. Let us stop being small-minded about men and freely acknowledge what treasures their obsessiveness has poured into culture.

We could make an epic catalog of male achievements, from paved roads, indoor plumbing, and washing machines to eyeglasses, antibiotics, and disposable diapers. We enjoy fresh, safe milk and meat, and vegetables and tropical fruits heaped in snowbound cities. When I cross the George Washington Bridge or any of America's great bridges, I think: *men* have done this. Construction is a sublime male poetry. When I see a giant crane passing on a flatbed truck, I pause in awe and reverence, as one would for a church procession. What power of conception, what grandiosity: these cranes tie us to ancient Egypt, where monumental architecture was first imagined and achieved. If civilization had been left in female hands, we would still be living in grass huts. A contemporary woman clapping on a hard hat merely enters a conceptual system invented by men. Capitalism is an art form, an Apollonian fabrication to rival nature. It is hypocritical for feminists and intellectuals to enjoy the pleasures and conveniences of capitalism while sneering at it. Even Thoreau's Walden was just a two-year experiment. Everyone born into capitalism has incurred a debt to it. Give Caesar his due.

The pagan dialectic of Apollonian and Dionysian was sweepingly comprehensive and accurate about mind and nature. Christian love is so lacking its emotional polarity that the Devil had to be invented to focus natural human hatred and hostility. Rousseauism's Christianized psychology has led to the tendency of liberals toward glumness or depression in the face of the political tensions, wars, and atrocities that daily contradict their assumptions. Perhaps the more we are sensitized by reading and education, the more we must repress the facts of chthonian nature. But the insupportable feminist dichotomy between sex and power must go. Just as the hatreds of divorce court expose the dark face beneath the mask of love, so is the truth about nature revealed during crisis. Victims of tornado and hurricane instinctively speak of 'the fury of Mother Nature' – how often we hear that phrase as the television camera follows dazed survivors picking through the wreckage of homes and towns. In the unconscious, everyone knows that Jehovah has never gained control of the savage elements. Nature is Pandemonium, an All Devils' Day.

There are no accidents, only nature throwing her weight around. Even the bomb merely releases energy that nature has put there. Nuclear war would be just a spark in the grandeur of space. Nor can radiation 'alter' nature: she will absorb it all. After the bomb, nature will pick up the cards we have spilled, shuffle them, and begin her game again. Nature is forever playing solitaire with herself.

Western love has been ambivalent from the start. As early as Sappho (600 BC) or even earlier in the epic legend of Helen of Troy, art records the push and pull of attraction and hostility in that perverse fascination we call love. There is a magnetics of eroticism in the west, due to the hardness of western personality:

eroticism is an electric forcefield between masks. The modern pursuit of self-realization has not led to sexual happiness, because assertions of selfhood merely release the amoral chaos of libido. Freedom is the most overrated modern idea, originating in the Romantic rebellion against bourgeois society. But only *in* society can one *be* an individual. Nature is waiting at society's gates to dissolve us in her chthonian bosom. Out with stereotypes, feminism proclaims. But stereotypes are the west's stunning sexual personae, the vehicles of art's assault against nature. The moment there is imagination, there is myth. We may have to accept an ethical cleavage between imagination and reality, tolerating horrors, rapes, and mutilations in art that we would not tolerate in society. For art is our message from the beyond, telling us what nature is up to. Not sex but cruelty is the great neglected or suppressed item on the modern humanistic agenda. We must honor the chthonian but not necessarily yield to it. In *The Rape of the Lock*, Pope counsels good humor as the only solution to sex war. So with our enslavement by chthonian nature. We must accept our pain, change what we can, and laugh at the rest. But let us see art for what it is and nature for what it is. From remotest antiquity, western art has been a parade of sexual personae, emanations of absolutist western mind. Western art is a cinema of sex and dreaming. Art is form struggling to wake from the nightmare of nature.

MARTIN AMIS · *God's Dice*
HANS CHRISTIAN ANDERSEN · *The Emperor's New Clothes*
MARCUS AURELIUS · *Meditations*
JAMES BALDWIN · *Sonny's Blues*
AMBROSE BIERCE · *An Occurrence at Owl Creek Bridge*
DIRK BOGARDE · *From Le Pigeonnier*
WILLIAM BOYD · *Killing Lizards*
POPPY Z. BRITE · *His Mouth will Taste of Wormwood*
ITALO CALVINO · *Ten Italian Folktales*
ALBERT CAMUS · *Summer*
TRUMAN CAPOTE · *First and Last*
RAYMOND CHANDLER · *Goldfish*
ANTON CHEKHOV · *The Black Monk*
ROALD DAHL · *Lamb to the Slaughter*
ELIZABETH DAVID · *I'll be with You in the Squeezing of a Lemon*
N. J. DAWOOD (TRANS.) · *The Seven Voyages of Sindbad the Sailor*
ISAK DINESEN · *The Dreaming Child*
SIR ARTHUR CONAN DOYLE · *The Man with the Twisted Lip*
DICK FRANCIS · *Racing Classics*
SIGMUND FREUD · *Five Lectures on Psycho-Analysis*
KAHLIL GIBRAN · *Prophet, Madman, Wanderer*
STEPHEN JAY GOULD · *Adam's Navel*
ALASDAIR GRAY · *Five Letters from an Eastern Empire*
GRAHAM GREENE · *Under the Garden*
JAMES HERRIOT · *Seven Yorkshire Tales*
PATRICIA HIGHSMITH · *Little Tales of Misogyny*
M. R. JAMES AND R. L. STEVENSON · *The Haunted Dolls' House*
RUDYARD KIPLING · *Baa Baa, Black Sheep*
PENELOPE LIVELY · *A Long Night at Abu Simbel*
KATHERINE MANSFIELD · *The Escape*

READ MORE IN PENGUIN

For complete information about books available from Penguin and how to order them, please write to us at the appropriate address below. Please note that for copyright reasons the selection of books varies from country to country.

IN THE UNITED KINGDOM: Please write to *Dept. JC, Penguin Books Ltd, FREEPOST, West Drayton, Middlesex UB7 0BR.*
If you have any difficulty in obtaining a title, please send your order with the correct money, plus ten per cent for postage and packaging, to *PO Box No. 11, West Drayton, Middlesex UB7 0BR.*

IN THE UNITED STATES: Please write to *Consumer Sales, Penguin USA, P.O. Box 999, Dept. 17109, Bergenfield, New Jersey 07621-0120.* VISA and MasterCard holders call 1-800-253-6476 to order all Penguin titles.

IN CANADA: Please write to *Penguin Books Canada Ltd, 10 Alcorn Avenue, Suite 300, Toronto, Ontario M4V 3B2.*

IN AUSTRALIA: Please write to *Penguin Books Australia Ltd, P.O. Box 257, Ringwood, Victoria 3134.*

IN NEW ZEALAND: Please write to *Penguin Books (NZ) Ltd, Private Bag 102902, North Shore Mail Centre, Auckland 10.*

IN INDIA: Please write to *Penguin Books India Pvt Ltd, 706 Eros Apartments, 56 Nehru Place, New Delhi 110 019.*

IN THE NETHERLANDS: Please write to *Penguin Books Netherlands bv, Postbus 3507, NL-1001 AH Amsterdam.*

IN GERMANY: Please write to *Penguin Books Deutschland GmbH, Metzlerstrasse 26, 60594 Frankfurt am Main.*

IN SPAIN: Please write to *Penguin Books S. A., Bravo Murillo 19, 1o B, 28015 Madrid.*

IN ITALY: Please write to *Penguin Italia s.r.l., Via Felice Casati 20, I–20124 Milano.*

IN FRANCE: Please write to *Penguin France S. A., 17 rue Lejeune, F–31000 Toulouse.*

IN JAPAN: Please write to *Penguin Books Japan, Ishikiribashi Building, 2–5–4, Suido, Bunkyo-ku, Tokyo 112.*

IN GREECE: Please write to *Penguin Hellas Ltd, Dimocritou 3, GR–106 71 Athens.*

IN SOUTH AFRICA: Please write to *Longman Penguin Southern Africa (Pty) Ltd, Private Bag X08, Bertsham 2013.*